The RESILIENT LEADER

Winslow Swart

Caitlin:
Yoroshiku
ウィンスロー
スワート

The Resilient Leader

By Winslow Swart

Cover Designed by Alex Swart

Kenseido® Press, 2010

13133 NW Military Hwy, Suite 200

San Antonio, TX 78231 USA

ISBN 978-0-578-06256-3

Acknowledgements

This book is written with gratitude to Tetsuo Hasegawa, my sensei in Japan, whose life-lessons continue to unfold and from whom I am still in the process of learning.

Sincere thanks to Harrison Evans M.D. and Bill Fry who originally helped to extract from me the core distinctions in mastery comprising *The Resilient Leader's* curricula in my early corporate training days.

Special thanks to my mother, Sonja Swart-van der Stam, who more than anyone else modeled the way of the Resilient Leader. By surviving three Nazi concentration camps in the Holocaust, and then going on to become a world-class athlete, mother, and brilliant artist, she showed us all the immense potential, power, and beauty of the human spirit.

In homage to my father, Hendrik Johannes Swart, of blessed memory, who fought, was wounded and survived several wars, embodied many of the life-lessons that come through in this book. An engineer with Hewlett-Packard, he was the consummate systems thinker and epitomized Resilient Leader traits throughout his life.

Thanks to Dean and Sandra Arteaga for their tremendous help on this project.

With sincere gratitude and appreciation for my family, my wife Pamela, and our five daughters for their love and support and for making this adventure called life really worthwhile.

The Resilient Leader

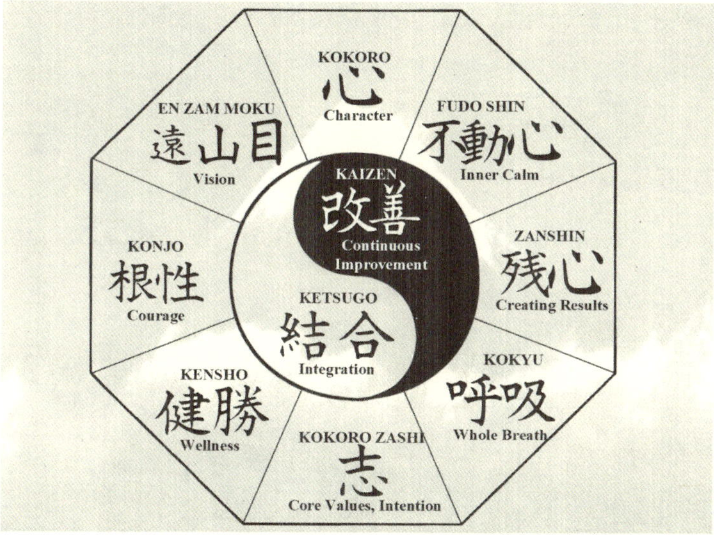

Distinctions in Mastery

Table of Contents

Kaizen

改
善

Prologue

改善

The Kaizen of Resilient Leadership

The Resilient Leader integrates the theories and practices of Kaizen with the distinctions in mastery learned in Budo (martial arts) like Kenseido and Kendo.

Kaizen is a management philosophy that focuses on continuous improvement. Kaizen is concerned with the idea that every input, process, and output must deliver value. While *The Resilient Leader* draws upon many of the elements of Kaizen, it is not a traditional Kaizen body of work.

The distinctions in mastery are the inner teachings and philosophy of Budo. These concepts include attributes of awareness, character, focus, internal power, and inner calm.

The fusing of these divergent notions — Kaizen and Budo — into a convergent body of knowledge provides a framework that has both personal and professional benefits.

Here is a little background on how this fusion of ideas came to be. The origins of Kaizen are known to most as being rooted in W. Edwards Demming's introduction of quality improvement systems to post-WWII Japanese industrialists. The common explanation is that Demming's ideas were rejected by American industry, but embraced by the Japanese captains of industry, primarily, because *they* knew they were in a crisis. The Japanese were trying to rebuild an economy against the backdrop of the rubble of WWII, having lost that war. This explanation is simplistic. The true story goes deeper than that.

Japanese industrial leaders were part of a class of society with direct lines to the Samurai, mostly clan leaders. The practice of Kendo, Japanese Samurai based fencing, was a part of their lives and daily regimen. Kendo is all about Kaizen, continuous improvement. It is also about something else. It is about resilience—drawing upon ones inner resources in order to overcome obstacles and barriers. This characteristic is known in Japanese as *Rinkyohein*: the adaptability to all circumstances.

At the time Demming came to Japan, the economic infrastructure was in shambles and they had no real natural resources of their own to speak of. So what did they have to draw upon in order to reinvent themselves? Obviously, some new theories on quality control, in and of themselves, were not going to be enough to pull the nation out of devastated circumstances. So what did it take for Japan to go from war-torn, wide spread poverty to become the world's third largest economy in just a little over two decades? It was a tradition of fortitude and resilience.

This tradition of fortitude, in spirit, is the subject of this book. *The Resilient Leader* presents a mental and spiritual disposition that draws upon the inner resource, provides the ability to draw upon this inner strength with unwavering concentration and inner calm, and that can be moved into action with blinding speed, if necessary. It also provides leaders with increased capacity to lead in the face of adversity.

The Resilient Leader also draws upon the concepts and practices of Kenseido. Kenseido is an art that amplifies human potential from the inside out. Kenseido involves both direct and indirect techniques and principles, which provides a framework for understanding how the dynamics of *yin* and *yang* principles occur in the arena of human experience. When properly directed this understanding serves as a vehicle for optimizing human potential.

The author distills the core ideologies of the eastern martial arts disciplines into an effective curriculum for developing leadership capabilities and increasing human performance. The lessons learned over the course of a lifetime of study, in the training halls of Japan, in the corporate boardrooms of America, the Netherlands, the United Kingdom, Mexico, and also Japan, and in the field of athletic competition, have crystallized into a deeply comprehensive source of inspiration and guidance.

The Resilient Leader guides today's leaders on both the inner journey towards personal mastery, and the outward journey towards professional success, and ultimately integrates the two paths. It demonstrates that success is a measurement of how well we transform obstacles into opportunity, overcome our barriers, and learn from both success and failure. The author has coached thousands in making the shift from victim to warrior, and from warrior to sage, as it relates to their daily work challenges, interpersonal conflict, and in transforming adversity into opportunity.

The process of breaking down internal and external barriers, and the dynamics for creating new results, is clearly explained in theory and in practice. Success stories, real examples (some action packed) and case studies where the model has proven effective, generate a vivid picture that will increase one's understanding and ability to put new ideas into practice. Leaders, who have successfully applied these lessons in the competitive arenas of both athletic competition, and in business, have done so with the use of these concepts and direct coaching of this author. NBA superstars, who changed their "inner game" in ways that resulted in a world championship, did so by using the tools within these pages. Entrepreneurs and senior executives faced with major strategic challenges, of daunting consumer markets, as well as corporate mid-managers confronting "burn-out" have found new ways to navigate success in rapidly changing business climates as *Resilient Leaders*.

The Resilient Leader builds upon the distinctions in mastery defined separately in each of the following sections. Each distinction in mastery enables the learner to change their internal environment and accomplish a "shift in being", resulting in the ability to positively impact and influence the events that confront them.

The distinctions in mastery that *Kyoshi Shihan* (a professorial designation in traditional Japanese Budo) Winslow Swart has distilled into a series of learning modules, increases one's ability to reduce stress, achieve inner calm, overcome fear, draw forth courage, vision, insight, innate wisdom, and to create the context for higher levels of performance, in work and in daily life.

These concepts and examples help make the cognitive connection from the inner to the outer self, and includes the disciplines of personal enrichment, maximizing the ability to meet and overcome daily challenges and exceed one's own goals and expectations.

The goal of *The Resilient Leader* is to provide readers with a profound understanding of their own potential for personal mastery, and a practical guide for optimizing their leadership capacity, in any arena of practice.

During the course of this book, the author will clarify the definition of each core concept, provide case studies and examples of how these concepts live, and in some cases, tools that can be used by the reader in order to learn how to apply these distinctions in times of need. The final section — *ketsugo*, or integration — outlines each concept with a short explanation, along with some additional frames of reference.

The Resilient Leader Training – Kaizen Module

In the *Kaizen – Resilient Leader* module, it is important to create a context and framework for continuous improvement on both personal and professional levels. By focusing on personal applications, attitudes and levels of awareness are more easily attuned, creating vital momentum, which, in turn, is more easily applied to the creation of a learning organization. In *Kaizen - Resilient Leader Training*, mind-opening scenarios help participants discover their own blind spots, and, armed with these revelations, find new ways to solve old problems. Creative, disciplined, innovative thinking invigorates leaders, as they are no longer distracted by "the way things are," and continually find new and better ways to live, lead, and produce.

Kokoro

心

Kokoro

心

Nakamura Sensei: The Lengths of Kindness

It was the winter of 1984, I was living in Kyoto, Japan, studying Japanese Budo (Kendo and Karate-Do) and the Japanese culture in general. As a twenty-four year old Black Belt from California, every day was like a dream come true. My grasp of the language was limited, though my interest in, and respect for everything I saw, heard, tasted, and learned was unlimited.

Most of my dojo training time took place in the afternoons and evenings, so I was free to explore early in the day. With over 2,000 Shinto shrines and Buddhist temples in the Kyoto area, I enjoyed countless architectural and cultural feasts for the senses. I would walk a different direction each morning making new friends and discoveries each day. Hada Sensei, a professor of Shinto studies at the International University in Kyoto, was also curator and resident of an 800 year-old Shinto shrine. There we would have tea and discuss the philosophies of Yagyu Sekishusai and Hon'ami Koestu.

He was very much like Koetsu. When his wife would serve us tea, she would do so purposefully, moving in between our thoughts or conversation, so you only realized her actions had taken place after the fact. In Japanese hospitality, this is called Kiku-Bari. In Budo (Kendo and Kenseido) it is called Shin-gan, a level of intuitive insight and awareness. Something learned after years training.

One day, I was walking in the direction of Takano shrine, a mountain Shinto complex several kilometers outside of Kyoto. I was stopped by a policeman who wanted to inform me that I now had entered the "Sugano prefecture." I still do not know why, but he seemed emphatic that I understood this. Some kind of warning that I thought would have been significant during the Tokugawa period. Later, I learned from my Japanese Kenseido colleague, Kasagawa Sensei, a Tokyo Police detective, that attention to detail is not just a cultural phenomenon, and that surveillance, for them is a way of life. Then something remarkable happened. While in the process of deciding which road to take at an intersection, an older Japanese man saw my confusion and offered to be helpful with directions. The extent of my Japanese and his English frustrated him. He then, very politely and gently, made the decision to ensure my safe arrival to my destination five kilometers away, by escorting me all the way up the mountain. He had a "shortcut" – a beautiful path that skirted a stream and the mountainside. This made it seven kilometers. Once I could see the thousand steps up to the shrine, he bowed deeply and then disappeared. Over the years and after many trips to Japan, these events, these moments of incredible kindness have occurred repeatedly. This aspect of *Kokoro*, of character, is a reoccurring theme in the traditions of Budo, Japanese samurai culture: a theme of service and selflessness.

A few years back I was taking the examination for Rokudan, 6th dan (master instructor red belt rank) in Kenseido, at Kashima in Ibaraki prefecture. My testing partner was Nakamura Sensei, a 55-year-old lifelong martial artist and also a student of my teacher Hasegawa-sensei. After an intense weekend of pushing one another to our limits, we returned to our respective abodes in the Tokyo area—he to the urban-center and me to the outskirts of Chiba.

Nakamura Sensei had taken several days off of work to attend the Kenshukai, Shihan camp, and was making up for it by working back-to-back double shifts at his two jobs. In the midst of that schedule, he had four hours of downtime when he could have gotten some much-needed sleep. Instead, he made a three and a half hour round trip to come out to where I was staying and present me with a small token of his esteem for having been his testing partner. The gift was small, thoughtful, and nice. The gesture, the effort, was huge. Although he acted as if it were no big deal, as if he was just passing-by, he would have felt remiss if he didn't express how he felt about what had just transpired between us. This is unusual behavior in most of the world, but not in Japan. It is Kokoro.

On the occasion of examining some Black Belts at my dojo several years ago, I called Hasegawa Sensei in Japan to get his approval prior. After reporting to him the merits of one of the students, Von, whom he had met, I went on and on about his skill level, dedication etc. Hasegawa Sensei thought for a long time, "mmmmm—-ahhh—-soooo—-mmmm," he began, and then, "Von-san …good kokoro…testing OK." This put everything into perspective. He was more concerned about the recommendation of the persons character, as the tangibles, at this point, were no longer in question. A few years later, when preparing to examine Alex and Gadier Senseis, I knew what to emphasize in the report…*kokoro*, of which they, fortunately, had plenty.

Kokoro refers to our inner resource. Identifying and connecting to inner strengths amplifies the capacity to elevate one's inner game and take performance and "being" to a higher level. Kokoro translates as heart, mind, soul, character, and essence. It is the prominence, connection to, and awareness of these attributes, that enables higher order thinking and higher order functioning, in Budo, in leadership, and in life.

The Resilient Leader Training – Kokoro Module

As Kokoro is about the leader's and the organization's core, this training module examines the conditions that can cause a disconnect (that which threatens or undermines) between the organization's core values and its ability to live into and fulfill its mission. Under duress, conditions may test a leader or a team's resolve and even upset the equilibrium. Through experiential training and rigorous dialogue, the team learns to recognize and confront inner opponents and meet shared challenges directly, transforming and elevating levels of ownership and accountability for the quality of the culture, and with increased commitment to shared outcomes.

Zanshin

残心

Zanshin

残 心

Umemoto Sensei's Sensei and His In-ability

Hiroshi Umemoto is the Kendo Kyoshi Sensei who advanced the kendo program at the Kenseido U.S. dojo into "Federation Style" Kendo back in 1990. At 71 years of age, Umemoto Sensei brought a lifetime of experience with him to every Kendo practice he attended. When asked of his experience, he would say, "I am just beginner, I have been practicing Kendo for only 50 years." When asked what that meant, in Kendo terms, he told a story about his teacher in Japan.

> *The dojo was almost exclusively filled with 6th-8th dan Kendoists, ranging from their late 40's to mid 70's in age. The premier Kenshi (swordsmen) of Japan, including several regional and national champions, were members at this dojo. After the usual warm-ups and keiko (sparring), a couple of the members left to go get "Sensei" so he could join the practice.*

Sensei would be napping, as it was midday. Knocking on the door, "Sensei... sumimasen... renshu desu neh...?" When Sensei finally got up, he needed assistance walking, as he was 90 years old and had trouble getting around. As he arrived at the dojo, he required assistance to get into seiza (sitting position on the wooden floor on the knees and shins), one Kenshi at each arm easing his descent. Then, due to rheumatism and arthritis in his shoulders, he required help putting on his bogu, (armor) and tying the himo (cords) of his men (helmet). Then, after mokuso, a few moments of breathing and meditation, it was time to draw the shinai (bamboo sword) and arise into kamae, fighting posture. Sensei rose as if on hydraulics, and then began to float across the floor as if on a cushion of air. When the shiai (sparring) began, Sensei bouted with several of Japan's most elite kenshi. No one was able to lay a sword on Sensei, when they tried he would somehow wind up behind them, his shinai crashing down upon their heads. "MMMMMMMEEEEEEEENNNNNN!!!!!!" (his Kiai, or battle cry) and then calmly, "...Sore ga kendo deuska? (Is this Kendo?) You can't even hit an old man?" This question was posed to 60 and 70 year-old Kendo masters, the best in all Japan—the irony was lost on no one. After several more unflattering imprecations and merciless "yuko datotsu" (valid strikes with his sword), Sensei returned to seiza for the end of practice mokuso. After mokuso, Sensei required assistance getting back to his feet, taking off his armor, and thus escorted by the two Kenshi, like two human crutches, back to his room to finish his nap.

The transformation that takes place for this elderly gentleman every time he participates in Kendo training is the purposeful summoning up of strength and willpower, qualities that are within each of us. The difference hinges on the ability to harness the massive potential of this inner resource in a manner we call Seishin and Zanshin. Seishin (next section) is a quality of being sometimes described as presence and bearing. Zanshin means "to emanate." This state is accomplished through a lifetime of exercises that require direct connection from the inner resource to that of creating outward results. Then, all aspects of being – physical, mental, spiritual, are fully present and actuated in a specific, focused manner. The transformation from feeble to masterful samurai becomes habit.

Umemoto Sensei passed away several years ago. He was the chief Kendo instructor for the Rocky Mountain Budokai in Denver. The story of his teacher in Japan was part of the way he taught Kendo, through examples and experiences. On separate occasions, Umemoto Sensei would write Japanese kanji characters for me in large dramatic brush strokes. After each kanji was finished, we would discuss each symbol's meaning as it applied to Kendo, and to life. Sometimes he would teach me how to write the character, and then relate the physical movement to the character's meaning and to Kendo technique itself. Kokoro or Shin (essence), Chikara (strength and/or sword), Ma-Ai (distance), Sachi (happiness), Koto-Buki (longevity), and i-Soku-i-To (one step, one-strike) were just some of the kanji and concepts we explored together.

One concept we discussed at length was Mu-shin, a transcendent concept that occurs after Shu-Ha-Ri (the transcending of technique upon complete mastery and internalization of technique). This transcendence is the fuel for future works to follow this book. Mu-shin happens when one is in complete harmony and a decisive action of the highest level occurs without forethought.

Takamoto Sensei, a Kenseido Shihan and lead *Kenshi* who teaches kendo with me at the dojo, and I still tell Umemoto Sensei stories to our Kendo students. His spirit lives on in us and in his perpetual influence.

The Resilient Leader Training – Zanshin Module

Zanshin is about creating and sustaining results. While initially planning and mapping a strategic plan with specific targets and goals is required, the process of "clearly standing in the future" takes place within Zanshin training as a mental, energetic, and physical course of action. In Zanshin, insurmountable obstacles are met both physically and mentally, linking the two in a dynamic and clear construct. The subconscious does not recognize metaphor, so the transformative, physical training that is clearly assigned to the individual and team performance objectives are embraced with both energy and intellect.

The outcomes of Zanshin training exercises have been startling. Over the years, literally hundreds of workshop participants have come back to me to report how their Zanshin experiences helped them transform personal and professional realities that have translated into very successful outcomes. These stories of achievement never cease to inspire me with awe and respect for every single human being's potential for greatness.

Seishin

精
神

Seishin

精神

Seishin and Konjo: Nanjo Sensei

Seishin is the ability to change the temperature in the room. It is the distinction that separates *being* from merely *doing*. It speaks to bringing a transformational level of passion and commitment to every task, action or deed. Seishin is when the qualities of being, those we often recognize as a reflection of a profound connection to our inner being, are fully present. From Seishin, emanates Konjo. Konjo deals with the ability to draw forth courage in the face of adversity. Overcoming challenges, breaking through barriers, and living into one's visions is also the function of Konjo. Konjo is visceral, it is felt.

Nanjo Sensei was not a tall man. Not even by Japanese standards. Nanjo Sensei was the Senmu Rigi, or most senior Shihan in Kenseido Japan, after the Doshu (Grandmaster) and Tani Sensei. When Nanjo Sensei passed away, he was succeeded to that post by my teacher Hasegawa Sensei. They were very close friends.

On the many occasions I had trained with Nanjo Sensei during my visits to Japan, a few things remain clear in my mind. He was a master of pressure point self-defense technique. Because of his very small stature, he would explain, he had to use every advantage available to him. So he mastered the art of exploiting the weaknesses of the human anatomy, even of the very strong. One evening after training, I was invited to join Nanjo Sensei for refreshments at an Izakaya, a casual bar/bistro that he owned. Sitting next to him in this eating and drinking establishment became a long and excruciating experience.

He proceeded, while speaking casually on all matters of daily life and martial arts, to exploit my physical weaknesses…twisting fingers, pressing vulnerable accu-points in a life-flashing-before-my-eyes manner. I can still remember his joyful laughter throughout. It was all without malice…I think. Now, in retrospect, I know I learned a lot from him, but at the time I just wanted to enjoy my nice Japanese beer after hard training.

A few years later I was in Japan with some of my students, including Dr. John Richardson. After "Nanjo Sensei Kenseido Dojo" training, we customarily joined Nanjo Sensei for refreshments at his Izakaya. This time, I graciously allowed Dr. Richardson the honored seat next to Nanjo Sensei. Sensei did not disappoint. Soon John's eyes were as big as dinner plates, unable to move, a chopstick pressed just behind his left ear. I had a very enjoyable, relaxing Japanese beer. It wasn't me this time.

Nanjo Sensei once told me, "Nine times out of ten, in all out combat, you would defeat me." He then explained why and described my physical advantages as a martial artist, speed, range, strength, size, etc.

Funny, the way he said, "Nine times out of ten…" makes you think that the *one* time in ten, the time that Nanjo Sensei would win, was in his mind, the only certainty. Nanjo Sensei was the epitome of courage. Size had never hindered his resolve or, in any situation, been an excuse. Now, whenever a student comes to me with the idea they can't do something because of one physical feature or another, I reflect back, and then help them work through those self-imposed limitations.

Naturally, my conversations with Nanjo Sensei would often gravitate towards the concept of Konjo, courage, and the important role it plays in Kenseido, and in life. One weekend, after such a dialogue, I was in the mountains of Japan with Hasegawa Sensei near Nikko and Kegon falls. We passed by a wood shop and something caught my eye. It was a wood burned plaque with kanji that held my attention. Hasegawa Sensei told me it said, "Konjo." I purchased it without hesitation and the plaque rests above my office door in the dojo, keeping the students and I mindful of Nanjo Sensei's life lessons.

The Resilient Leader Training – Seishin Module

The Seishin module is about a shift in being, or more accurately, shifting from merely to "doing" towards increased levels of "being." John Adams' quote, *"No amount of human doing, or human having, can make up for a deficit in human being,"* sums up the idea. However, for a shift to occur and be sustainable, training exercises that go beyond language are required. Such exercises allow participants to learn from the experience of an authentic "shift in being." Anchoring learning exercises to individual or shared challenges not only helps bring about a reorientation, but also ensures that it sticks. The result is increased levels of personal confidence, particularly in areas where the participant may have struggled previously.

Fudoshin

不
動
心

不 動 心

Fudoshin: Reflections of a Kyoshi

The smell of drying tatami mats, the numbness in the feet and knees, smoke wafting in from an incense cauldron, distant sounds…monks chanting, wind through the bamboo, a city coming alive in its own language, then nothing. A soundless echo. Time adrift.

Later that morning, I walked through the suburban hamlet of Sakae-machi, as shopkeepers washed down storefront sidewalks amidst the polite scurrying and rhythm of daily commerce. The morning mokuso-session at Narita-san temple had a strong lingering effect—an inner sense of calm. Good thing too, as that weekend's Shihan (Kenseido master) examination and training would challenge my very core. A nice cup of sencha at the corner tea shop allowed additional time for contemplation.

A great sense of well-being brings a smile.

This is the way one should feel, always, even in the midst of great trials – but we don't. How do we allow ourselves to become so fragmented? Is there any reason why this sense of *enwholement*, of connectedness, cannot be a constant?

Fear, anger, stress – these negative, undermining emotions and strained behaviors have an antidote. It is called Fudoshin: to be the calm in the eye of the storm, possess and maintain inner calm and focus in the face chaos, adversity, and conflict.

There is a method and a process for accomplishing such a sense of inner calm and peace. There are techniques, skill sets, competencies — distinctions in mastery — that lend themselves to the capacity for Fudoshin. It is the result of training and experience. But what kind of training? What kind of experience? Let us explore both.

The story goes like this: Two high ranking Shihan's were discussing their struggle with achieving inner calm through meditation. The higher ranking of the two, in his frustration said, "I am nothing. I just cannot achieve the state of pure awareness that will bring me to a place of complete Fudoshin."

His kohai was dismayed, "But Sensei, if you are nothing, then I, who am many years your junior, must really be nothing." The uchi-deshi, a beginner student who is charged with o-soji, the cleaning of the dojo, overheard this conversation and approached the two Shihans, "My esteemed teachers, if you are nothing, then I, who know very little, must REALLY be nothing!" The Shihans looked at one another in disbelief and the younger of the two rebuked the uchi-deshi saying, "Who are you to be nothing?"

What is the evidence for arriving at a state of Fudoshin? It is often realized when one has overcome an insurmountable psychological challenge. Usually it is recognized in a situational respect, when one has been at the other end of the spectrum, the opposite end of calm. In sharp contrast to a sense of inner peace, when one's equilibrium is in danger of being completely upset and a realization that the consequences will be extreme as well. What kind of consequences?

Failure, of any kind.

From an individual living a life of stress and unhappiness to an elite professional athlete who, mysteriously, cannot find his groove and whose performance and livelihood are at risk. A law enforcement officer or soldier whose judgment gets clouded and fear overwhelms his confidence in the heat of battle. A key-note speaker who becomes distracted by an audiences non-verbal cues of incredulity. A person who can't get to sleep at night. A leader lacking in a sense of purpose and vision. Anxiety induced illness. Perpetual self-medication. The inability to overcome interpersonal communication barriers or life's set-backs. The inability to be in the moment and appreciate life. In contrast, much can be understood. The process of de-fragmenting one's emotions, thoughts, and awareness, opens the path towards clarity of mind and calmness of being.

...exhaling like a cool mist, aware of sounds, light, thoughts, but not distracted by them. Observing the sound of one's own breathing, pulse, heartbeat and then...stillness...another random thought, a sound then...more stillness...noticed in retrospect...where was I for a minute? Ahh yes, meditating...how cool...

That which comes easy, is not a test for transforming one's state of being. What comes easily, comes easily, what does not can be insurmountable, particularly when the approach is externally based. When struggle exists and adversity arises, Fudoshin is a powerful tool.

I have noticed when I am required to "go into battle," a metaphor I use for facing the greater challenges in life, it is a call to align and integrate my inner resources in a deliberate manner: focusing and centering, namely through the disciplines of Mokuso and Kokyu (meditation and internal breathing exercises). Through the practice of quieting the mind and the internal dialogue, everything falls into place. Stillness is then followed by a clear sense of mission and purpose. Now, seemingly insurmountable tasks are endeavored with greater ease. Stacks of concrete bricks are broken (that used to be my signature demonstration) with an exhale and a percussive touch of the palm. Grand visions for personal and professional success are realized as struggles dissipate. We learn how to get out of our own way.

...breathing in through the nose, cooling through the sinus, holding at the depths, breathing out, slowly...colors swarming inside of eyelids, an amusing light play, then...

There are two dispositions from where this is not easily appreciated:

- Those for whom things come easily, and there is no need for confronting obstacles, either real or perceived
- Those who insist that difficulties are derived, largely, from outside of themselves—rephrased—the persistent belief that stuff happens to us, and we are not in control of any of it

The power of context applies here. In a harmonious physical environment or inner state of tranquility, all is well and everything flows, and there is no need for further attention toward inner clam. In a state of belief persistence and struggle, some pre-work is required before Fudoshin can be seriously considered.

...exhales with dynamic tension from the lower abdomen and almost isometric-ally, through the bronchia, the

exhale....sounds like Darth Vader breathing...Zanshin breath welling up the sense of ki, internal energy, and calm, focused, prepared...

Our locus of control may shift throughout the day, and throughout periods of our lives. Noticing this, when it occurs, is key. If we listen in, it says, "Get settled, get clear, and get focused." If we ignore the signs or insist on looking outwards for resolution the struggle becomes more consuming. We become spiritually incendiary – burning up our own ki (internal energy). When your locus of control is internal, you are calm. When it is external you may either fight for control, become resigned, or retreat. Neither, from the perspective of clarity, nor of *The Resilient Leader*, is a winning strategy. The "fight or flight" response is a strong human tendency. The techniques needed to transform these physio-emotional states toward higher order thinking, and being, are quite simple, the discipline to do so is not. Because the notion of "don't just do something, sit there!" seems so antithetical to an appropriate response, we naturally resist.

...time stood still, and at the same time flew by. Even, absent was the sense of place...

Fudoshin: what is it and how do you get there? While the process is dynamic, non-linear and can be spontaneous or deliberate, there is not just one path towards this profound sense of inner calm and awareness. It should also be noted that we are not discussing a purely passive state of tranquility, but one that can be converted into deliberate ready action, this is a true state of Fudoshin.

The following sequence, though quite compressed, may be helpful in seeing how the separate distinctions in mastery inter-relate:

Begin with Kokyu, profound breathing (anywhere from 3 to 300 breaths, depending upon your level of mastery) to bring about the sense of *mokuso*, meditation, without actually meditating. Then, bring forth a powerful sense of *seishin,* of presence and bearing, through more dynamic breathing, but not too amplified, as the sense of calm should not be disturbed. Now, a dimension of *En Zam Moku,* of simultaneously looking and seeing is required, not on the ocular level, but the conceptual, which is more *shingan*, seeing with your spirit. From here, the sense of your surrounding is acute, but not agitated, and the breathing continues. To activate Fudoshin into an external focus is called Zanshin. When this happens spontaneously it is known as Mushin. So here you have the crux of thousands of years of martial wisdom and over forty-some years of training and study in one paragraph. Sounds simple enough. Be mindful that these are just words, and there are limits to what can be expressed verbally. The experience and the discussion of Fudoshin, are only similar on a conceptual level. It is the continued practice of "doing" that will lead to higher levels of understanding and "being."

When you have mastered your craft, so that you can effortlessly repeat a seemingly impossible skill, over and over, this is quite good. Doing so under duress, fatigue, strain or pressure, in less than ideal circumstances, is where the sense of Fudoshin comes in. This is the training of the samurai. The un-distractible zone. The next level. This is where my Kenseido and Kendo students, who learned to succeed in the post-season in the NBA, in the courtroom as trial attorneys, as corporate athletes and individuals overcoming physical, mental, psychological and emotional barriers do in fact succeed in the game of life, in a way that inspires a sense of awe when reflecting on those many accomplishments.

...infinite calm, where no thought of self or action occurs...a final exhale, eyes now open, the opponent visible...greater in stature than imagined. Then, imperceptibly, the opening becomes clear...quickly slipping into the crease in his awareness, the match is finished before anyone realized it had begun.

The Resilient Leader Training – Fudoshin Module

Fudoshin training is a confluence of at least two other modules and then put into a practicum of its own. Fudoshin is about being "the calm in the eye of the storm," and the process of getting there is alluded to in this section. The first step is to master Kokyu, a profound breathing technique that allows the individual to dissipate stress and begin to clear the mind. Almost all negative emotions and stress responses will be associated with shallow, distressed breathing, and this module helps go to the other end of that spectrum.

Once profound breathing has been mastered, it becomes possible to achieve profound stillness through the practice of Mokuso. Mokuso is meditation. The techniques used in Resilient Leadership Training are practical, easy to learn and have been readily embraced by a wide range of cultures and people of different orientations. This process is a precursor to implementing all of the other distinctions in mastery at their highest possible levels.

En Zam Moku

遠
山
目

遠 山 目

En Zam Moku: A Samurai Point of View

The idea of vision has far reaching applications, both conceptual and corporeal. In En Zam Moku, we consider and examine both extensively. Consider these vision statements:

> "Become the company most known for changing the worldwide poor-quality image of Japanese products."
>
> \- Sony's vision statement , 1950 -

> "We will crush, squash, and slaughter Yamaha."
>
> \- Honda's vision statement, 1960's -

These statements reflect the power of a clear vision and, at the same time, the limits. The inner dynamics of vision have been explored for thousands of years. The En Zam Moku model can provide some helpful insights on levels both personal and shared.

En Zam Moku exemplifies the two-fold gaze of sight and perception. It is both looking and seeing at the same time. The physical, ocular aspect is known as small-scale-strategy or tactic. Large-scale strategy is found in applying the concept to the greater, more comprehensive issues in life. This perspective comes from Miyamoto Musashi's treatise "The Five Scrolls."

The applications of this concept are limitless and can be brought to situations both practical and conceptual. Literally, En Zam Moku means to view the distant mountain, and it is implied, simultaneously the ground at your feet. There are techniques practiced in Kendo and Kenseido that exercise the eyes and the mind to do just that.

There is a truism (in my way of thinking) that applies to both the martial arts practitioner and the organizational leader: if you don't have En Zam Moku, you are going to get hit, as there will invariably be blind spots. With En Zam Moku, you become *unhittable*. Relaxed, responsive, alert, ready, and focused. The sharper your En Zam Moku, the closer you can get to your opponent while deflecting their every move, and the better equipped you are to deal with operational challenges as well.

The martial artist cannot afford to look at the movements coming at him. It is not possible for the eye to adjust and focus at that rate of speed, at near distance. So one must learn to diffuse one's gaze, look past one's opponent and see everything. Similarly, a leader cannot get drawn into daily minutia. She has to keep her focus connected to the organization's mission and vision, while simultaneously managing daily operational issues.

In large-scale strategy, En Zam Moku is invoked at the planning stage. The "looking" component is applied when assessing the current state of the organization, its values, and competitive strengths—its core. The "seeing" component allows leaders to raise their heads above the tree line and envision their organization's future. Combing the two perspectives into an En Zam Moku practicum is the key to living into the declared vision.

While there are other disciplines at work, in concert, like the distinctions of Kokoro-zashi (values driven) and Zanshin (results oriented) for example, En

Zam Moku is the guiding discipline for maintaining individual and organizational focus.

...hands moving in an arc, from above the head, and along the circumference of the arc, down towards the knees. Far back they are held, to very edge of the periphery, while eyes held fast on a distant point ahead. See the hands as they move, while focusing on the point in the distance, do not let the eyes waver, keep the breathing slow and continuous...

Then...

...continuous chain-linked punches thrown by one participant towards their partners face, the recipient- calm expression gazing into the distance, breathing deep and slow, circular open-handed blocks moving inwards. The punches speed up and so do the kakete-style blocks, the breathing remains rhythmic and the expression calm...

Applied...

...a junior executive walks out of the board room at Citibank moving his hands in an inward, circular manner as if swatting flies. A tic? A spasm? Gnats? "Mike what are you doing?" "I'm practicing my En Zam Moku. What

happened in there, I can handle just fine if I remember what we learned in that leadership seminar. I used to get so stressed out in these meetings, now I am seeing a much bigger picture…."

En Zam Moku lends itself to rich coaching opportunities equipping recipients with the ability to successfully manage conflict. Connecting the present moment or tasks with a larger and more comprehensive awareness makes resolution seem effortless.

Modern psychology has a theory (Albrecht) that 93% of all communication is non-verbal.

A martial arts case study:

…Somehow, his intention became known to me, what he was planning, his next strike. Preemptively, I initiate the counter before he goes into motion. Although there is no time to think, I realize halfway through the action, my intuition is accurate. More fun than the landing the shot is the look of surprise and dismay on my opponent's face. "How do you keep doing that?", he wonders. "Are you reading my mind?" No. I am not reading your mind. I am reading your spirit…

A lot of what we think and believe is the result of having filtered out some of what we perceive. When what we perceive doesn't line up with what we want to think and believe, we filter some of it out. There is a natural resistance to even the smallest degree of change. By creating a context that rules out this resistance, one can engage in completely open and honest perception. The martial arts are a great laboratory for developing this trait. Applying it in other environments is the real test.

By taking the mental awareness and physical feeling derived from En Zam Moku and bringing it to other contexts in life, both personally and professionally, one may experience a shift in the depth to which sensory data, in other words, vital information, becomes evident and realized.

...There was no time to stretch or prepare. I had been busy judging the lower division matches when the last call was announced for the advanced ranks. It was a regional championship. Usually, participants get to warm-up and stretch. No time, compete now or forfeit. One very deep calming breath with a long, dynamic exhale allowed my gaze to settle on middle distance. Ready...hajime! The next thing I remember was being declared the winner, my

opponents scoreless. Playing it back in my mind, a vague recollection of seeing the opponent as if frozen in mid-technique, and the realization that contact had been made, repeatedly...

The Samurai have this theory of intuitive vision called Shingan. This is a dimension of En Zam Moku that can, on occasion, be accessed organically, but as a discipline it can be replicated at will and is the result of much training.

If En Zam Moku is about expanding ones aperture and not getting hit, then Shingan is about seeing an opening, whether it appears to exist or not. By asserting a position with clear vision one can more easily realize, even obscured, opportunities upon which you are free to seize and execute strategy. *The Resilient Leader* does not say, "We are successful at our firm because our competition is weak" but rather, "We prevail because it is our way."

Takamura Sensei (my Kendo teacher from 1993 to 1997, who lives in Kamakura, Japan) taught:

"...when practicing Mokuso, meditation, do not let your eyes close, but keep the lids open, just enough, so a diffused view is visible, just as you diffuse your hearing, you should diffuse your gaze. This will teach you to be calm and to see with your mind..."

The Resilient Leader Training – En Zam Moku Module

En Zam Moku is about vision in the most comprehensive sense. Learning through both the mind and the body provides leaders and teams with context-changing learning experiences that deepen and broaden their own relationship to the creation and realization of shared visions.

In En Zam Moku, participants learn the same envisioning techniques that were taught to the samurai, and then concentrically apply this knowledge to personal, shared, and then organizational vision creation and challenges. Once the techniques have been anchored through the shared learning process, individual resolve is heightened and, as a result, there then exists a shared language that serves to fortify the group's focus and resolve.

Kokoro - Zashi

志

Kokoro - Zashi

志

Hasegawa Sensei: A Life of Value

Hasegawa Sensei has always been more than a great Shihan. He is the moral compass for many in a society consumed with the concept of right action and a person whom the other top-level Shihans can go to for guidance. They know he lives his values *all* of the time which is especially revered in a culture where a lapse of "right action" easily results in *hazkashii*, embarrassment and/or disgrace. What unique kind of person can serve as the "values police" for those living in a values-driven culture?

After Nakahashi Sensei (my first Kenseido teacher) moved back to Japan early in 1990, I was left with the key-role of leading Kenseido in the U.S. My frequent presence in Japan became imperative. After an incessant program of Kenseido dojo hopping throughout the Kanto region, Hasegawa Sensei finally "adopted" me. This was not a small matter. Beyond his concern for the future of

Kenseido in the U.S., there were two basic tests that would occur over time, along with several trips to Japan. One test was my willingness and ability to adopt "Yamato da Mashii" or a traditional Japanese way of thinking as it pertained to duty and relationships. The other was surviving training at Hasegawa Tokiwa Daira dojo - the most severe training throughout the Kenseido system.

For most of my colleagues, even those in Japan, one trip to Hasegawa Sensei's dojo was more than enough. Very rarely would anyone make a second trip. I proved to be an exception. I kept coming back. Finally after a few years and several return visits, I became a member of this select bunch, able to train and match intensity in their excessive manner. My classmates (we are all 5th, 6th and 7th degree master instructors) refer to this idiosyncrasy as "O-kashii"- literally: funny, but in a humorous way it means a bit mental. Who would want to continually subject themselves to the unforgiving full-contact version of Kenseido?

There are plenty of welcoming dojos in Japan providing solid training and high-level technique, and without the concern for one's own physical well-being at each and every practice. This is what can only be described as old fashioned. You see, Hasegawa Sensei's dojo emphasizes Kokoro—heart, mind, and spirit. Their belief is that the only way to develop these attributes is by pushing one another beyond their physical limits. Interestingly, this treatment is seen as the ultimate kindness: to be in service of one another, helping to improve inner and physical strength by challenging one another to rise to the occasion.

In sharp contrast to what may seem an overly excessive training environment, are the kindest, most generous and giving people you will ever meet. Hasegawa Sensei takes the responsibility for extending Japanese-style hospitality quite seriously. With samurai-like vigor, when you are his guest, you are completely his guest! A vivid example, and also one of contrast, is the first time I was struck by my Sensei outside of the dojo. I tried to pick-up the tab at an eatery in Tokyo. "Crack!!!" went one of my cervical vertebrae, having been struck with an ippon ken (a single knuckle fist*)* followed by, "Don't try that again." Old school.

The next time "I tried that again" was a few years later in the mountains of Nikko. I had four of my students with me and figured I would pay the tab while Hasegawa

Sensei excused himself for a moment. When he returned, the plan was for everyone to say that they had paid, creating confusion and hopefully, just an awkward social situation. No go. They were my students; I was their Sempai (senior) and ultimately the responsible party either way. Picture a middle-aged Japanese man in pursuit of a 6'2", 215 lb western man in the middle of a resort area with Japanese tourist onlookers. Low kicks, *swoosh*, barely missing my legs, me scurrying down a forest path in retreat, Hasegawa Sensei voicing imprecations under his breath all the while. Kinda' funny, now in retrospect.

It's still all about context, however. The training is never limited to the dojo when Sensei and Seito (teacher and student) are concerned. When the training is complete, there are ways that you will be informed. The Sensei is in service of the student, though it doesn't always seem that way. Because of *budo no kankei*, the unique, powerful bond and the *giri* and *gimu*, profound duty and obligation that goes with it, a teacher like Hasegawa Sensei does not take on too many direct students. The old ways require great personal sacrifice.

On one of my first visits back to Japan as Beikoku so Hombu-cho, leader of U.S. Kenseido, Hasegawa Sensei and his class of Shihans took up a cash collection in order to present me with O-Rei, a gift of money for a distinguished traveler, which is a tradition among samurai pre-dating the Tokugawa period (16th c.). A mizuhiki (intricately decorated envelope) labeled with the kanji "O-Rei" was filled with a stack of 10,000-yen notes ($100 bills). I had read about this, though had never envisioned being a recipient and am still a bit overwhelmed by the honor, 20 years later.

After all the visits to Japan, and all the time I have spent with Hasegawa Sensei, I have rarely been allowed to pay for anything in his presence, and the exceptions were clear: gifts for others, special items for the dojo, and purchases that were not customary. When entertaining all of the Japanese Sensei's who have come here came to visit us in San Antonio, Texas over the years, we have tried to extend the same kind of hospitality.

Customs around the world are unique, and it does not always make sense to adopt foreign practices in a vacuum. It is the generosity of spirit, however, and the character traits that focus on strengthening the other learned in Budo, that *is* transferable to the American culture, or any other culture for that matter.

The following personal story mirrors one of legendary samurai lore, though my version is a bit more humorous in nature. The original story is of Yagyu Muneyoshi when he was attempting to master the technique of Muto (literally, without sword), a level of skill and awareness that makes the need for the katana (Japanese Sword) obsolete. Muneyoshi charged his student with the task of attacking him anytime, anyplace, with a live blade, even in the middle of the night on his way to the bathroom. This he practiced successfully. The goal was to sharpen his awareness and to develop Mushin, the state of perpetual, unconscious awareness.

The daily, ongoing training concept works well in Japan. Students do not expect to be given preferential treatment at anytime. Sneak attacks, to help improve awareness, and incidentally, to provide comic relief, is a way of life. In Japan you do not go to bed until your Sensei is ready to retire. If you have jet lag, tough. When you are finally “dismissed,” you are out like a light.

This custom feeds well into Hasegawa Sensei’s nighttime-ninja-ambush-attacks, executed while you are all snuggled, comatose in your futon. I have been his makiwara (striking post) many the times. The last time it happened, was some years back. I was in my futon in the guest tatami (straw mat) room nodding off, when I detected the faint sounds of socks on the stairway. Not even a creak, really. I quietly rolled out of the futon and backed up to the tokonoma (decorative showcase).

Silently the shoji door slid open. Hasegawa stepped lightly onto the tatami, then rising up into the air, came down onto a pile of bedding, fist landing, unexpectedly, onto the floor. From behind, my kiai and controlled attack surprised him and much laughter ensued. "Zamamiro!!!!! Got you this time!!!" I think Sensei enjoyed that as much as I did.

When I was just a 4th and 5th dan, being berated was still a part of life with Sensei. That finally changed, but I remember the glory days as a second-class citizen. Sixteen years ago, Hasegawa and his wife Misao came to visit us in Texas. After several days in the dojo teaching our students together, we went down to Port Aransas, Texas, a barrier island, along with my wife Pamela Sensei (now a 5th dan), who also trained with Sensei in Japan.

The beach condo was ideal, and after a full day of activities, we were lounging about watching TV, relaxing.

The Hasegawa's were treating me to a shiatsu session, pressure point massage. Somewhere along the way, I must have seemed to be enjoying this treatment a bit too much for my rank, (you see, my training was not yet complete) and the massage became pressure point treatment of the excruciatingly painful martial kind! All of the points on the body used for healing and preserving life can also be used for taking life away.

With the two of them working my extremities, I was unable to escape, so it must have sounded like an off-the-grid torture chamber, with the exception of my wife's laughter in the background. "Gaman! (Endure!) More strong after." OK, I get it already. All-in-all, pretty funny stuff, well at least almost everyone was laughing.

Actually, most of the coaching I received from Sensei, outside of the dojo, was by example and through verbal instruction. Only occasionally, was I treated to a nice dose of martial arts hazing. Pretty normal behavior in Nippon. The nice thing is, Sensei is always up for receiving a lesson as well.

Mrs. Hasegawa is a treasure. The students refer to her as "Saiko Shihan" great teacher. It took me a while to fully understand why. She grew up near a Buddhist temple in Nishi-Arai, polishing the wooden floors, gates and ancient doors, and learning the traditional heirloom arts of Japan. Her brother, Takkai Kasuya, whom I also had occasion to study with, is still a part-time monk there as well as the Sou-Shihan of Kenseikai. Takkai Sensei honored me with the rank of 5th dan in his system. Their life growing up was one of rigor and beauty.

One day we were in a *depatoo* - Takashimaya department store in Kashiwa - maybe four of us *Shihans* or so, and Misao-san. She was dressed impeccably, her fashions reminiscent of Jacqueline Kennedy. As the elevator ascended, Mrs. Hasegawa began to lean and push us, ever so slightly, back into the corner of the elevator with her back and arms. The four of us were increasingly being squished, as she was leg pressing the opposite wall of the elevator. We were unable to move, she had leveraged the situation just right, us pressed to the wall, she fully braced against the other end.

As the elevator opened, Mrs. Hasegawa abruptly stepped out of the elevator, having released the compression she had us pinned with. Suddenly, four grown men were tumbling and sprawling out of the elevator like bowling pins, and onto the 4th floor of Takashimaya *depatoo* - house wares. That is the surprise that greeted the cluster of unsuspecting, elevator-waiting, Japanese shoppers. They even had to jump back to avoid our tumble of humanity. And Misao-san? Nowhere in sight.

Ten aisles down past the formal china she was, hand held daintily to her mouth in order to obscure her chuckle. As we recovered from our disheveled embarrassment, picking ourselves up, the lessons were dizzying. What technique! What strategy! What a sense of humor! Excuse me Mrs. Hasegawa, can I help with dishes? Perhaps take out the trash? Carry your groceries? Saiko Shihan!

Fun story aside, Mrs. Hasegawa has the spirit of kiku-bari, much like Hada-san's wife in Kyoto. The ability to intuit your next desire, thought, or request. This is often compared to the attribute of Shingan, discussed earlier. When it comes to hospitality, her attention to detail is awesome. She is also a welcome participant and counsel when it comes to matters on a more global level.

Shihan meetings without Misao-san are missing an important perspective. She too, is a beacon we can set our moral compass to.

Another study in contrast, where the kind and generous meet the severe and relentless, is Sato Sensei. When I first met Sato Sensei at his dojo in Misato, in Saitama prefecture, I saw only his back, which was only the width of a Japanese tractor-trailer. He was punching and kicking the makiwara (striking post) in his dojo before class, just enough so that the building would tremor. No wait, not a makiwara, but the concrete supports of an 18-story building of which the basement housed the dojo. Enough to cause it to tremor…mmm…?

The children showed up and Sato Sensei beamed with the biggest smile you have ever seen. Throughout the entire class he beamed. Smiling and training, that was Sato Sensei. After all, this room is also the kindergarten classroom where he is the teacher during the day. Next up was the adult class. "Shuuuugooo!!! (Line-up!)," his voice thundered.

Here is this Japanese Arnold Schwarzenegger looking guy in a red belt glaring at us as we begin warm-ups. He really means business…and here we go. What happened to that smiling, jolly, Japanese Santa Claus looking-guy that was here a few minutes ago? Another fine pushed-to-our-physical-limits-experience that would have worried me, but the jet lag and rigorous training schedule was so overwhelming, I didn't have time to notice. Adult training completed, once again appeared the smiling Ho-tei, the jolly monk of lore.

Sato Sensei had a parting gift for me: oddly, a Louisville slugger baseball bat. But just at that moment…on cue, two black belts take the bat, one on each end, held against their shins. A quick step and Sato Sensei breaks it with his shin. He is a low kick expert. There is film of him breaking four of these bats at once. I take my souvenir without fully internalizing the warning.

A few years later, I get into a low kicking contest with Sato Sensei at Shihan camp. A shin-on-shin exchange of kicks until one of us surrenders. There was that smile again, but this time for entirely different reasons. To this day, there is a whole section of my shin that is without feeling. Super nice guy, though.

Hasegawa Sensei comes from a culture of stewardship. Not all Japanese, his age or younger, have this so deeply ingrained. There are plenty of folks in Japan today who point directions versus taking you there, who go "Dutch" versus picking-up the tab, take friendships lightly, and are more self-oriented than others-oriented. Call it globalization. Sensei calls it a lack of Budo.

No matter the circumstances, or the context, from Hasegawa Sensei's point of view, it always comes down to Kokoro, character. Not just what you think, or what you say, but what you do. Who you are. This is Kokoro-Zashi. Living your values. Everyday, all of the time. Maybe this isn't always the case. Perhaps under duress, we shift away from our core, a little bit, and then a little more. With resolve, determination and practice, our habits and behaviors can better reflect our core, perhaps all of the time.

Today, being true to your core may very well be the definition of Samurai.

The Resilient Leader Training – Kokoro-Zashi Module

Kokoro-Zashi is the articulate expression of the inner qualities of Kokoro. It is described as will, aim and intention. It is also described as core value. In Kokoro-Zashi training, individual and shared values are identified and explored as well as the conditions that disconnect one from their values.

Participant teams become even more values driven, as they learn how "not to struggle" and "get out of their own way," In addition, a process that clearly maps where everyone has been, is now, and may ultimately be going, provides a unique compass for personal and professional navigation.

One's core values may be the most powerful force for resiliency and sustaining a meaningful course in life.

Kensho

健
勝

Kensho

健 勝

Kensho - Wellness: A Kaizen Approach

I set the earthenware bowl down on the table and declared, "Gochiso sama deshita!" in gratitude for the excellent meal. Hasegawa Sensei looked down at my bowl and frowned, saying, "Zannen!" Too bad. "Kawaiso," It's a pity, echoed Mrs. Hasegawa. "Doshte?" Why, what do you mean? I asked. "The farmers," explained Sensei, "all their toil and hard work throughout the year. Planting and replanting, braving the seasons and the elements." You see there was a little bit of rice left in the bottom of the bowl. And they looked upon those kernels with deep remorse, as if an entire lifetime had been wasted, spent in vain.

When wellness is considered, it often concerns diet and nutrition—of eating, in the biological sense. Yet, are all of the other wellness aspects surrounding food properly considered? What of enjoyment, and appreciation? What of environment, culture, spiritual aspects, and eco-systems? Muda, to be wasteful, is antithetical to Kaizen and wellness. So perhaps, in order to expand the definition and awareness of the whole concept of wellness, consider not just what is consumed and when, but also where people co-exist on the food chain, physically and spiritually.

Having a healthy approach to wellness implies that one can have an unhealthy approach. Holistically thinking, this is of great importance in the area of wellness. The mind plays a significant role in overall health and wellness throughout life. So, if you are determined, exert a great deal of energy and worry about every single calorie, will you be healthy? Not for certain, but you may become mentally ill in the process.

Research on the attitudinal aspects of wellness are quite compelling - just the stress factors alone can be quite debilitating. Of course, it is not the only factor. In addition to one's mental and emotional state, there is diet, exercise, environment and genetics. All of these but the last are controllable. The degree to which genetics determine your state and level of health is the subject of much research and debate, but since it is largely "uncontrollable" we will focus on the other aspects.

Some Kaizen of wellness coaching:

The Kaizen of wellness is about continuous, even incremental, improvement—making a habit out of doing things just a little better, and over time, garnering a series of small, achievable wins and ultimately, a formula for success. The idea of "kakushin" break-through, dramatic, revolutionary change does not always succeed when it comes to lifestyle habits and choices. The exception is when there has been a cathartic event that shocks the organism and psyche into change. Health events, like heart attacks that say, "change your ways or else" for example.

Here is a dietary basic. If you want to look like a sumo wrestler, then eat like one. Feast on large meals at the end of the day. If not, do the opposite. I won't say much more about food, except that I love it. I have developed a healthy gourmet way of life that is enjoyable and I do not stress out about the notion of "diet." You've gotta' do what works for you, for your metabolism, your actively levels, your culture and your palate. Getting to where it works for you, your health and your enjoyment is the key to sustainability. And don't forget about your people –family, friends and community. Kinda' hard to be an island, so being inclusive is also a recipe for sustainability.

Kaizen is also about value. If you value what you are doing on all levels, there is more built-in reinforcement and reward. You can always improve from there.

In Kaizen, there is an effort to reduce waste (muda) strain (mura) and defects (muri). What is the strain on your system, i.e. your body and your psyche? Genchi genbutsu (the place of truth) is the idea of finding the root cause of a problem. If the root cause is something deeply ingrained, or something you would be very reluctant to give up, then finding it is all the more difficult. Injuries, illnesses, fatigue, and stress are indicators of strain, and these are the things that stand in your way. This is the discipline part of Kaizen, since once things become a good habit, it's hard to call that discipline. Finding the truth and challenging whether an old habit adds value, that is Kaizen. Once discovered, the course is clear.

Exercise? Workout? Ha! You mean treadmills, weights, fitness classes, ugh! Now a clear vision emerges of ambitious goals and well-crafted excuses, mostly related to time starvation and, "I tried that but had to quit because…" Of all the physically engaging activities, what do you REALLY want to do? What accessible forms of recreation do you enjoy enough to do regularly? What have you always wanted to do? Remember your mind and heart are going with you for every workout, so it's a good idea to make everybody happy if there is going to be any hope for success.

Here are some thoughts to be mindful of when considering and developing a wellness plan: appreciation, enjoyment, discipline, others, environment, tranquility, invigoration, joy, self-sacrifice, more joy, accelerated moderation, fun, consistency, spontaneity, dabble, mastery.

Now, choose one minor thing to improve in your own wellness regimen, right away. Next, plan your big, major improvement objective and begin taking a few small steps towards that end. Now you have momentum. Maintaining this inertia will keep you smiling, on the inside.

The Resilient Leader Training – Kensho Module

The Kensho, or wellness module, helps leaders look comprehensively at their own "physical portfolios." With a Kaizen approach towards wellness, the so-called "value-stream" does not end with the self, but is conscious of the eco-systems, environments, and individuals that are affected by one's choices and behaviors. In this way we are not solely concerned with a model that contributes to individual resilience, but also the sustainability of the model over time.

Ketsugo

結

合

Ketsugo

結　合

Ketsugo – Integration

Ketsugo is not to be counted as a distinction in and of itself. To be mindfully aware of the importance of internalizing and integrating all of the distinctions in mastery through practice and achieving an appropriate balance of internal and external awareness is a function of self-coaching.

Here, in this section, all of the distinctions in mastery included in *The Resilient Leader* are compressed into useful explanations, so that your own strategies and practices for putting-it-all-together can brainstorm and develop into a plan of action.

Kaizen - Continuous Improvement

改善

Kaizen means continuous improvement and is typically associated with the philosophy that gave birth to Total Quality Management (TQM) and Total Quality Control (TQC). As a leadership discipline, Kaizen focuses on the *human equation* and is concerned with individual continuous improvements and even kakushin, (breakthrough, transformational learning). It is no coincidence that the early adopters of Kaizen, the captains of Japanese industry after WWII, were also practitioners of Kendo, Japanese fencing.

The discipline of Kendo, embodies Kaizen through the way it fosters personal mastery and this approach is further elucidated herein, given greater clarity in the context of providing relevant applications for *The Resilient Leader*.

Kokoro – Character, Essence, Heart Mind, Soul

心

Kokoro refers to the inner resources that can translate into elevated "inner game" abilities. Identifying and connecting to our inner strengths amplifies our capacity to elevate our "inner game" and take performance to the next level. Kokoro translates as heart, mind, and soul. It is the prominence and awareness of these attributes, and the degree to which they simultaneously occur that result in higher order thinking and being. Much of the attention throughout this study is to recognize what separates us from these qualities, and the process of connecting or re-connecting to these core strengths.

Kokoro Zashi -Will, Aim, and Intention

志

Kokoro Zashi is the outward manifestation of Kokoro. Kokoro is the innate human quality we all, by our very nature, possess. Kokoro Zashi is the unique way in which those qualities become evident, and identifiable in the form of the core values that drive us.

En Zam Moku – Vision

遠 山 目

En Zam Moku in the Japanese language, describes the two fold gaze of perception and site. Literally, or in the context of small scale strategy, En Zam Moku distinguishes between merely looking and seeing. In terms of large-scale strategy, it denotes the relationship between personal, shared, and organizational vision.

Seishin – Presence and Bearing

精 神

Seishin is the ability to change the temperature in the room. It is the distinction that separates being, from merely doing. It speaks to bringing a transformative level of passion and commitment to every task or challenge. Seishin is when the qualities of being, that we often recognize as a reflection of personal mastery, are fully present. From Seishin, emanates Konjo. Konjo deals with the ability to draw forth courage in the face of adversity. Overcoming challenges, breaking through barriers, and living into our visions is the function of Konjo.

Fudoshin - Inner calm

不 動 心

Fudoshin is about being the calm in the eye of the storm. Being impervious to distraction yet fully aware, even amidst chaos, is the function of Fudoshin. Clarity of mind and emotional calm are attributes needed to succeed in a volatile business climate, and this also prevents the erosion of our enthusiasm for our work and invigorates the energy levels we can sustain throughout our lives. Fudoshin, which literally means the inner calm of the soul, refers to being the eye in the calm of the storm.

It is from this state of awareness that a Samurai acts with blinding speed, impervious to distraction. It is the place from where true creativity and vision can emanate. Fudoshin, is devoid of stress, anxiety and fear. Mastering Fudoshin enables people to function at a higher level while under duress or when resolving conflict.

Fudoshin, a pivotal quality in advancing personal mastery, is a vital step in the process of becoming a *Resilient Leader.*

Zanshin – Creating Results

残 心

Zanshin means "to emanate." When we focus and direct our character attributes to emanate, we have a dramatic impact on events and the results we create. Zanshin is the vehicle for eradicating fear and self-imposed limitations while creating outward results.

Kokyu - Internal Breath

呼 吸

Kokyu is the function of dissipating stress, and enabling the distinctions of Zanshin, Fudoshin, En Zam Moku, Konjo, Kokoro, Mokuso and Kensho. The simple act of continuous conscious breathing facilitates higher functioning on both physiological and cognitive levels.

Mokuso – Stillness

黙 想

Mokuso is the discipline of meditation. For driven, high achieving professionals, the most difficult thing is to do absolutely nothing. Counter-intuitively, this can sometimes be the most important thing to do. A few well executed moments of profound quiet can yield incredible rewards of vitality and vigor, and increase productivity on all levels.

Kensho – Wellness

健 勝

Kensho is the discipline of investing in your physical portfolio as a strategy for sustainable success. With a Kaizen approach to wellness, continually improving all aspects of physical health serves as a source, and as a reflection of our inner health.

Additional Concepts

Hei Ho – Strategy

兵 法

Hei Ho is, in Japanese, the title of Sun Tzu's treatise "The Art of War," or "The Art of Strategy." The study of Hei Ho enhances leaders' ability to recognize patterns and opportunites and to postion their organizations for success. The Art of Strategy, historically, has been required reading for the Samurai and is also an important source of guidance for the *Resilient Leader* of today.

Waza – Technique and Tactics

技

There are many types of waza, or techniques, that teach and inform one how to use internal energy, physicality and mental capacities in order to maximize one's resources and not to overly exert oneself needlessly, without benefit.

In the spirit of Sun Tzu's strategic thinking, Zhug Liang (2nd century C.E. China) provides an example of tactical thinking, that is also used as a form of situational guidance, in this adapted brief below:

1. **Thoughtfulness** - using agents for intelligence
2. **Organization** - gathering news and watching carefully
3. **Courage** - not being disturbed by opposition or events
4. **Modesty** - thinking of justice and duty when seeing the opportunity for gain
5. **Impartiality** - being egalitarian in matters of reward and punishment
6. **Forbearance** - being able to bear setbacks
7. **Magnanimity** - being able to accept the population, tolerance of diversity
8. **Trustworthiness** - so there can be serious cooperation
9. **Respect** - honoring the wise and able, respecting diversity
10. **Clarity of Mind** - not listening to slander, not contributing to the rumor mill
11. **Reason** - not forgetting accumulated experience

12. **Human Kindness** - taking care of those for whom you are responsible
13. **Loyalty** - devoting oneself to the organization
14. **Moderation** - knowing to stop when you have enough of anything
15. **Planning** - assessing yourself first and then assessing others
16. **Responsibility** - leading the acquisition of resources and skills and breaking down barriers
17. **Intuition** - trusting your innate sense of right and wrong and acting upon it

Whenever confronting conflict, or an impasse with another, in business, or in daily life, consider two of the insights listed above and a solution may then be more easily forthcoming. Select two advices from the list above that seem like opposites, or are counter-veiling in nature, as this offers the most balanced approach.

The Resilient Leader Training – Ketsugo Module

In Ketsugo, the integration module, personal strategy maps for increasing resilience and success are developed utilizing all of the distinctions in mastery learned throughout Resilient Leader Training. Various matrices are designed contingent upon individual, group and organizational needs. It is often best to design leadership development plans around shared performance objectives, and within action-oriented models. This approach creates tangible targets and mutual accountability, which is far more effective than leadership development programs conducted within a vacuum of self-interest.

About The Author

教士師範

Kyoshi Shihan Winslow Swart

Spanning three continents and a wide range of industries, Winslow Swart's work with executives, managers, and teams has improved leadership acumen, performance, and work flows in areas where people and process intersect and often collide.

He holds a Masters Degree in Administration and Organizational Development and a Bachelors Degree in Psychology of Organizations and Development. Currently pursuing a Doctorate in Management and Organizational Leadership, Winslow lives what he teaches: life-long learning and continuous improvement-practical Kaizen.

Winslow dedicates himself to helping his clients create strategic, high performing leadership cultures, enabling them to outperform their peers both in areas of quality and business performance.

Winslow Swart was the first non-Japanese Shihan of Kenseido in the world. A Shihan is professorial rank in traditional Japanese “Budo" of which Swart Sensei holds a 6th degree in Kenseido, and a 7th degree in Kenshindo. Swart Shihan is the direct student of Kenshindo’s Sou-Shihan - Hasegawa Tetsuo and the Dosyu of Kenseido - Akizuki Takayoshi, for whom Swart is the chief representative in the U.S. Winslow Swart also has Dan level ranking in the Japanese fencing art of Kendo under the Zen Nihon Kendo Renmei and the All U.S. Kendo Federation.

Mr. Swart established the U.S. Headquarters School of Kenseido in 1986 and continues to facilitate Kenseido's growth in the U.S. Shihan Swart has studied martial arts for over forty years, much of that study in Japan.

Winslow is also a dedicated husband and father of five young learners.

Online Resources:

www.winslowswart.com

www.kenseido.com

The applied categories for *The Resilient Leader* are:

Business Management

Leadership

Self Improvement/Self Help

Philosophy

Psychology

Spirituality

Martial Arts

Sports Psychology